I0486352

Making $40,000 per Month in Extra Income

A Step-by-Step Guide in Building Wealth through Various Income Streams

Marc Gaudet

Disclaimer

The income amounts presented in this book will vary between each individual and are not guaranteed. We are not responsible for the outcomes of your techniques attempted as part of this guide. The cash inflow streams outlined in this manual are only meant for supplementary income and should not be relied upon as your sole source of income. Income amounts will depend on various factors including effort and time spent on building income generating opportunities. In addition, some practices explained in this book may not be applicable in the country where you reside. All income amounts presented are stated in US Dollars.

TOPIC CONTENTS

"Do you want to be safe and good, or do you want to take a chance and be great?"

- Jimmy Johnson
Dallas Cowboys Coach

Preface

My Previous Life

First, I would like to thank you for purchasing this book and taking a chance. I hope once you have finished reading this book, you will not have any regrets. My goal is to expose you to different income generating ideas that will help you achieve a better and more comfortable lifestyle.

I had been working for five years after college and my salary was on the rise but so was my debt. At one point, I had over $35,000 in credit card debt – which has now been paid off as a result of the methods in this book. I had more debt after working five years than when I first came out of school! I am sure you know the feeling as well. On top of all this, my expenses had gradually increased with the desire of trying to acquire better and bigger goods to keep up with others.

I tried to set aside what I could afford after watching way too much personal finance television shows that would guarantee me to be a millionaire before retirement. They claimed this can **only** happen if I stop my $5 daily lattes and put $5 a day in my savings account and let it grow for 15 years. Don't worry this book is **not** about giving up your lattes or waiting 15 years until financial comfort!

I became obsessed with reading and learning more about personal finance. I worked hard to build a solid base both in my investment account and my retirement account. However, due to the stock market plunge, most of my investments had **EVAPORATED**! With no savings and trying to pay off my debt, I could honestly say, I was living pay check to pay check.

Similar to most people, I hated my regular 9 to 5 (more like 9 to 8, 9 or 10) job as I felt too old to be brown nosing through the rat race yet way too young to retire – I was only 28! I felt trapped and all I could think about at work was how to make more money outside of work. On top of all this, my employer reduced 20% of the workforce causing an unstable work environment. I needed alternate means of income in the event my primary income stream was cut!

I refused to get a part-time job, after all, it seemed like everyone was making more money at home or online. I started exploring various ideas by reading online articles, books, and talking to various individuals through networking. I even clicked on various internet ads that promised "Executive Pay" for only hours per week. Most turned out to be scams that had nothing to deliver.   However, I did find some methods quite interesting as each taught different ideas to developing your income streams.   Through all these resources, I selected key practices that I catered to my needs. You too can do the same.   One unifying factor that I have learned is to automate all your supplementary income streams so you can still maintain your primary income.

Having studied Business in school, I knew the market volatility could have less impact on your personal life if you have diversified streams of income. **Don't keep all your eggs in one basket.** But how does one get to this point?   I started merging ideas of diversification with what I learned through my research to make alternative forms of income. I continued to read more about personal finance and ways to secure constant income flow.   This served as a basis for what came ahead in my life.

My life started changing as I practiced some of the techniques I came across and became more comfortable with the additional income resulting from the techniques.   Now, I am able to treat myself to the luxuries in life that I only once could dream of. I'm able to take unpaid time off (which my boss loves since it saves costs for the company) as I no longer rely on only one income source. Just this past year, I have traveled to 17 countries – mostly in Business or First Class for pleasure!!

So, what if I said "Diversifying Your Income Streams Leads to Increased Wealth"? It could be true and possible! It was for me. What about "Thousands of Dollars per Month in Supplementary Income"? These are bold statements. However, with today's ailing market, you need to find other sources of income to supplement your primary income.

In the content that follows, I will present various opportunities for you to develop and earn additional income. Through all my previous research, I have compiled, in my opinion, methods that **anyone** can implement to earn additional income. Some methods will require little to no start up capital and some will require more substantial investment capital which we will work towards or which some of you may already have. In any case, I have presented various ideas in which you can try according to your ability and comfort level.

"The person that turns over the most rocks wins the game. And that's always been my philosophy."

- Peter Lynch
Successful Wall Street Investor

Introduction

Developing Your Income Streams

As I mentioned in the Preface, I explored many options of various income streams. This guide provides a brief overview of the methods that I have come across to be the most effective as alternate forms of income. In developing your income streams, I suggest following the order as presented in this book. This will gradually increase your comfort zone so you may progress to each new level. As you will see, it is not difficult to set up these methods.

Many also require little to no time to maintain so the income streams will complement your current income. However, as you read this guide, try to picture yourself setting up each channel before proceeding to the next to prepare yourself mentally.

I have also included a "**Let's Get Started**" section in each of the income channels to provide a basic step-by-step guide on how you can start your income flow.

"Success seems to be connected with action. Successful people keep moving. They make mistakes, but they don't quit."

- Conrad Hilton
Hilton Hotels

Chapter 1

Become an Affiliate

Becoming an affiliate requires little to no start-up costs and has the potential to generate income with little maintenance work. Basically, you promote a product that has an affiliate program through the internet and if someone purchases the product through your promotion, you will earn a percentage of the sales or a commission. Some programs will offer up to 75% of the sales price – that is $75 per sale on a $100 product! Sellers of these products would like to use as many channels of sales as possible which is why they pay such a high commission rate.

First, you will need to find an Affiliate Program Network which will provide you access to a listing of products that offer an affiliate program. Once you have the product selected, the affiliate program will provide you with a link that is unique to your account. If buyers purchase the product through this link, you will get paid.

Consequently, to drive buyers to the product through your link, you will need to advertise the product. There are various and effective ways to advertise the product through the internet that are free or low in cost. In my opinion, the most effective and FREE way to advertise is to write an article about the product and send it out to as many ezines, websites that host articles, classifieds, forums, and even blog sites.

Let's Get Started:

- Find an Affiliate Program Network or go to ClickBank (**www.clickbank.com**) and signup for a free account. Many have said ClickBank has the most favorable payouts and most popular products. There are also over 10,000 products for you to choose from through ClickBank. You will require a unique nickname or login username – you will later use this to generate your unique link to promote the products.

- Browse through the various products that offer affiliate programs. If you are using ClickBank, click on "Marketplace" near the top of the homepage. Also, ClickBank will provide the amount the affiliate will pay you should someone purchase the product through your link. You can find products by category, popularity, or highest paying affiliates.

- **TIPS:** When selecting a product, you should consider a product that you have interest in. This will make it easier for you to write an article about and promote. Also, consider the payout rate; ensure that the payout amount will achieve your goal.

- Select your product and generate your affiliate link (also known as a "hoplink"). For ClickBank, once you select the product, click on "create hoplink". This link is how your affiliate network tracks the sales that were referred by you. A pop-up window will ask you to provide the nickname that you created in the first step. The "Tracking ID" is optional and not required; this will just allow you to track where your sales are coming from. For example, you can have a tracking ID of "Craigslist" – you will then use this on all your Craigslist ads (**www.craigslist.com**). You can then generate another tracking ID of "article" for the same product to use specifically for all your links you will submit as an article. Later, you can then compare which channel drives more sales in your ClickBank account and place more focus on advertising efforts in those channels.

- Write an article to promote your product or to convince others why they should purchase this product. Be confident in the article to make you sound like an expert.

- **TIPS**: Also, try to sound like you are reviewing the product so that people don't think it is advertising.

- Advertise your product for FREE by posting or sending your article to websites such as: **www.Craigslist.com, www.Kijiji.com, www.Wordpress.com, www.Articlecity.com, www.ezinearticles.com**, etc. Perform an additional search on the internet for free advertising channels. You can also start a discussion on various **message boards** and include a link to your affiliate product. This will generate some exposure to draw buyers to your product.

- You can also create your own website or blog and advertise through those channels. More will be discussed in later chapters but I'll give you an overview here. You DON'T need to be a website expert to implement this! Trust me, I am living proof! For information on how to create your website, refer to Chapter 2 in the "Let's Get Started" section, paragraph 1. There are many websites that walk you through the process of how to create your own website. Perform a quick search and you will find many. I used WordPress (**www.wordpress.com**) for one of my sites and created my first website in two hours. If you plan to use the income stream from Chapter 2, you may want to consider using a different free website provider as WordPress does not allow the tools required in Chapter 2.

- You can type up your promotional verbiage and then include a link to your product and put up some images to attract more people. There are also other free website tools that I have listed below in Chapter 2 - "Let's Get Started" section, paragraph 2.

- Many resources recommend that you get your own unique domain name, such as, www.yourdomainname.com. However, this will cost you $7 - $15 per month. You can explore this option once you become familiar with the income generating tools and are ready to build a more complex website.

- On your website, come up with a theme that unifies the products from your affiliates. Write posts or pages that talk about topics that relate to your theme and modestly incorporate links to your affiliate product. This way, your website does not seem like pure advertising – quality content will bring traffic.

- Another advertising channel is ebay. The only barrier with ebay is that you have to create a Classified Ad to attach your affiliate product's link. The cost of listing a Classified Ad on ebay is $9.99 for 30 days. If you think you can recoup this with your sales, then this is a good idea. However, this is an initial investment that you may risk. The largest benefit of ebay is that you have access to millions of buyers around the world. If you decide to try the ebay route, do a search to find the most searched ebay words and try to incorporate this into your title.

In my case, once I selected the product to become an affiliate of, I spent approximately 2 hours writing the article with the link and another 1 – 2 hours per week emailing the article out to various channels. I also wrote reviews on the product and posted this on my website under a page called "Money Saving Recommendations". I had quite a few clicks in this section – I would imagine the phrase "Money Saving" caught some attention.

The product I promoted offered $40 per sale in which I managed to sell on average 10 units per month. This provided me with a total of approximately **$400** per month! As I got more familiar with the system, I was able to identify which advertising channels provided more traffic by using a "tracking ID" (mentioned above) on each avenue. I focused my efforts on these channels and increased sales to **$600** per month.

My friend who found a product that paid $85 per unit and sold an average of 100 units per month for a total of $8,500 per month! Of course, he spends much more time advertising his product on his numerous websites. The point is that your income potential depends on how much time you would like to spend promoting your product.

Also, see John Chow's website in Chapter Four and how he managed to earn over **$12,000** per month from affiliate income.

"Have a bias toward action - let's see something happen now. You can break that big plan into small steps and take the first step right away."

- Indira Gandhi
Former Female Prime Minister of India

Chapter 2

Google AdSense Like Crazy

This form of income stream may seem modest at first but has a multiplying effect when used in different ways. Once you have learned the basics of this technique, you will be able to expand it to methods explained in Chapters 3 and 4 to take full advantage of this tool.

Google AdSense is a form of advertising in which YOU will get paid each time someone clicks on the ad. Google will find the advertisers for you and find the appropriate advertisement for your homepage to maximize your sites revenue potential. You just have to supply the space on your website. The advertisement content will be matched to your website content by Google so you just collect checks once you have implemented AdSense to your site. It is pretty much automatic!

Sounds a little too good to be true? Well, this is how it works. The advertisers will bid for space with Google, for example, an advertiser bids 75 cents for each ad placed. If you allow the advertising space for the ad, Google will pay you approximately 30 – 40 cents for every click make on the advertisement. Google will take their share but gives you a percentage of the advertising revenue.

Remember, **you ALREADY have a website** from above! However, I have listed additional resources and tools in the "Let's Get Started" section below to help you build more websites if your time permits. The more websites you have, the more potential income you can receive. Also, the second "Let's Get Started" section will show you ways you can increase traffic to your site.

Let's Get Started:

- Go to Google AdSense (**www.google.com/AdSense**) to sign up for a free account. You will access this later once you have created your websites.

- You can create additional websites using: GeoCities (**www.geocities.yahoo.com**), FreeWebs (**www.freewebs.com**), Wix (**www.wix.com**), SquareSpace (**www.squarespace.com**).

- **TIPS:** If you are having trouble thinking of content to put on your website, consider the following categories as different pages of your website: **About Me, Posts or Articles, About the Website** (or reasons why it was created), **Random Thoughts, Resources** (perhaps a good place to recommend your affiliate products that may relate to your website), **Travel, and Latest News.**

- Add Google AdSense to each of your websites. To do this, login to your Google AdSense account that you had setup. Once you have logged in, near the top, you will find some blue tabs. Click on "AdSense Setup", then "AdSense for Content". You will now be able to select your format and color of ad you want. Follow the remaining instructions on Google to complete the setup process and add AdSense to your site.

What is the use of having a website if there is no traffic? The goal is to try and build traffic to your site and have people follow your website and start clicking on the ads!

Driving Traffic to Your Site
Let's Get Started:

- Index your site with Google so your site will come up on search engines. Go to Google (**http://www.google.com/addurl**) to allow your website to appear on search engines.

- Do the same with Yahoo (**http://search.yahoo.com/info/submit.html**) so your site is searchable on Yahoo.

- It can be difficult to drive traffic to your site so we want to ensure you send out "pings" or notifications that you have a website. Go to Ping-o-matic (**www.pingomatic.com**) and follow the instructions to ping your website. Some website host providers may have the pings automatically sent for you.

- You can use a pay per click advertising service. Basically, your website will show up as an advertisement on other people's website. You will have to pay and bid on whatever price you can pay for visitors to be directed to your website based on keywords you select. HOWEVER, see Chapter 3 for another income idea.

- Go to various message boards and post comments to attract people to your site. Ensure the message boards allow you to post links. If you can't post a link, ensure you tell message board readers that they can email you or private message you through the board for the link to your website.

- Another free method of driving traffic to your site is writing articles as mentioned above.

- **TIPS**: It has been said the following topics for websites and blogs yield the most traffic: **Making Money, Technology, Health & Fitness, and Celebrities**. It may be a good idea to add these topics for content to your website.

I will be honest; AdSense has not been my biggest money maker. However, the primary benefit of this tool is that it's very low maintenance. Referring to John Chow, he achieved AdSense revenues of **$3,000** in September 2008 which he admits is only 10% of his revenues.

However, if you get creative, you can generate significant amounts from this method. Perhaps the largest AdSense check that has been issued came close to **$720,000** in June 2006 by Markus Frind, CEO of a free online dating site Plenty Of Fish (**www.plentyoffish.com**). The actual check was for $901,733.86 CAD (using an exchange rate of $1.25 CAD = $1.00 USD, yields an approximate value of $720,000 USD) which covered a period of two months. An interview with Markus Frind and an image of the actual check can be found on WorkHappy.net (**http://www.workhappy.net/2006/06/interview_ with_.html**). Markus continues to make $25,000 per day off AdSense revenues!

Along the same lines as Markus, you can really earn top dollar. Consider creating a social networking site, free dating site, or a membership site and earn money on your advertising. I know building a website such as this may get complex, but if you have the idea for content and just need technical assistance in executing the website, you can hire cheap experts. Find freelancers on sites like Craigslist (**www.craigslist.com**) or Elance (**www.elance.com**) that charge reasonable prices. Although you may not have the capital to hire technical help yet, keep this option in mind for later.

"A book holds a house of gold."

- Chinese Proverb

Chapter 3

Spreading it Between What Comes in and What Goes Out

Ok, this part might get a little tricky, however, there is a potential to earn more than the income you made in Chapter 2. So now you know with Google Adwords, YOU pay people to come to your site (also known as pay per click ads or PPC ads). And with Google AdSense, GOOGLE pays you for people to visit their ads. The interesting concept is that in general, AdSense PAYS YOU MORE than what you will pay for pay per click ads! Why not become the broker or "middle-person" so that once people click to come to your site, lure them into the AdSense ads? You will EARN THE DIFFERENCE IN ADDITIONAL INCOME! Note that there are many smaller pay per click search engines that you can go to and bid on cheap traffic to your website. Generally, these will be cheaper than Google and allow you to have a larger profit. Plus, using Adwords to drive traffic to your site just to show people AdSense ads may be against Google's Terms of Service.

Be warned however. You still need to maintain good website content that is of value to your visitors – otherwise, they won't return! Also, try to update your content regularly. For me, this is quite hard as I often had no idea what to put on my website (plus, I'm lazy). If you run into the same problem, try searching for different articles available on the web that allow for republishing. You can then add the content to your website and just reference the source. Frequent updates will often lead to more traffic allowing you to better profit on the spread.

Let's Get Started:

- Find cheap small pay per click ad service providers by performing an internet search. Use keywords such as "PPC search engines". Start bidding for your ads to drive traffic to your site. Please read the terms and conditions of each provider before setting this up as some providers of both PPC and advertising do not allow you to drive traffic to your site only to have them driven out.

- **TIPS:** Before you sign up for the pay per click services, perform another search for online coupons to lower the cost you will pay for clicks. If the timing is right, you may be able to find $50 off coupons for these services.

- On your website, upload as many Google AdSense ads as you can. Google will automatically ensure the ads are relevant to your website enticing your viewers to click on their ads.

"Money is not the most important thing in the world. Love is. Fortunately, I love money."

— Anonymous

Chapter 4

Blogging Like You've Never Known

Alright, you may not believe it when I say you can make up to **$38,000** from your blog. But you can! And here is the evidence: In 2006, a guy named John Chow started a blog called "John Chow dot Com – Miscellaneous Ramblings of a Dot Com Mogul" (**www.johnchow.com**).[1]

He did a case study to see if he can earn a full time salary from only blogging 2 hours a day. In his first attempt at building his blog, he made $353 in September 2006. As he promoted his blog through the same methods mentioned in this book, traffic increased through the year. The following year, the blog income had hit $20,512!! In September 2008 it had reached $38,000, with almost $15,000 in his earnings from the first two income streams I have presented earlier. The remaining **$23,000** of additional income earned that

[1] Source: John Chow dot Com, www.johnchow.com, September Blog Income Report (September 2008)

month was through his custom blog. At this rate, he is expected to earn over $400,000 a year in blogging! Follow the techniques closely and your dedication can also turn into **$400,000** a year!

Let's Get Started:

- If you don't already have a blog, go to Blogger (**www.blogger.com**) or any other blog website and sign up for a FREE account and build your blog. Ensure your blog provider allows Google AdSense to be added so you can maximize your additional income.

- Once you have signed up, click on "Create Your Blog Now". You can take the article that you already created above in Chapter 1 and post it to your blog. Place some content about yourself in the "About Me" section – and there, you have yourself a Blog! If you prefer to use other blogging sites, you can also consider these networks: **OnlyWire.com, Google, Digg and Yahoo**. Whichever network you decide to join, ensure the network is large enough so you have access to a large group of visitors.

- **TIPS:** Don't forget to add AdSense to your blog! If you decided to use Blogger as your blog service provider, Blogger should ask you if you would like to add Google AdSense. However, if not, just click on "Edit Post", scroll to the bottom of the page to "Tools", and click "AdSense". You should be able to follow the instructions to add AdSense to your blog.

- Go to John Chow's website (**www.johnchow.com**) and read the September 2008 archived Income Report post to see tips on how to build your blog and start on the road to **$38,000** per month!

- Post on your blog often!

Bringing more visitors to your blog is key! Like we did with your website in Chapter 2, we want to bring traffic to your blog. You can also use the same techniques mentioned in Chapter 2 to increase traffic to your blog, however, review the additional methods below to bring more traffic to your blog.

Driving Traffic to Your Blog
Let's Get Started:

- As mentioned briefly earlier, studies have shown that the following topics will bring on average more than 150 visitors per day: technology, making money online, health, and celebrities. This is something to consider when trying to achieve more traffic to earn more income!

- On your website you created earlier, create a link to your blog; this will bring additional traffic to your site.

- Add tags on your posts. Tags are words or phrases that are associated to your post and will allow your post to be searched by search engines based on the tag you have attached.

- A good method to drive additional traffic to your site is to write comments on other blogs with a link to your site. Perform a search of other top blogs that have the same topics as your blog. Place a customized comment with a link to your blog on these top blogs. These top blogs already have high traffic volume so you want to use their site as an opportunity to promote your blog. If you don't customize the comment, your comment can be classified as spam and be removed.

- Use your "Blogroll" – basically a Blogroll manages links to your favorite websites. Contact the owners of the top blogs you found in the point above. Tell them how much you love their site and ask them if they can include a link to your website if you add a link to theirs on your Blogroll. This will benefit you in two ways: (1) increase traffic to your site and (2) ncrease your PR score. We will discuss PR score more in the next Chapter. This will benefit them as visitors from your blog can visit their site and may increase their PR score. If they need more convincing, advise them that you will write a passage that will rave about their blog on yours.

- If you prefer just to link to other blogs without contacting the owner, you can also link to other blogs by leaving a trackback on the other blog to let them know you've linked to their blog. Blogs that allow trackbacks will include a link back to your blog in the comments section of the post that you originally linked to. People do click on trackback links[2].

- Submit your best posts to social networking sites such as Digg (**www.digg.com**), StumbleUpon (**www.stumbleupon.com**) and Reddit (**www.reddit.com**).

- If you have a Facebook (**www.facebook.com**) profile, add your blog or website link to your Facebook profile.

- It is a good idea to make a slight investment here to bring even MORE traffic to your blog and website. John Chow was so successful because his blog caught so much attention. One way to catch the attention is to issue Press Releases! A Press Release is like an article but will guarantee

---

[2] Source:
http://weblogs.about.com/od/bloggingtips/tp/TipsIncreaseBlog Traffic.htm

attention on Google News, Yahoo News, Newswire, and AOL. A Press Release will cost you about $30 to $80 depending on which agency you go to. Here are some good agencies: PR Free (**www.prfree.com**), e-releases (**www.ereleases.com**), PR Web (**www.PRweb.com**). Write the Press Release with any content you want – which is great since all you have to do is promote how great your website or blog is! This is your chance to promote your website and drive traffic to your site. More traffic means more clicks on your AdSense ads and potential buyers from your affiliate partners.

- Remember to update your blog often so your followers will start talking about your site in forums. I try to post consistently (twice per week) to ensure my followers keep coming back. I added a travel section to my blog so I just add a few pictures every trip and I'm done! This way they keep checking your site for new content while your ads are still running in the back.

- Nominate your blog to the various blog awards available. Perform a search of these awards online and nominate yourself. Although you may not win, this will definitely draw additional attention to your site.

"Twenty years from now you will be more disappointed by the things you didn't do than by the ones you did. So throw off the bowlines, sail away from the safe harbor, catch the trade winds in your sails. Explore. Dream. Discover."

- Mark Twain

Chapter 5

Text-Linking Low Down

Text-Link Ads are similar to Google AdSense but instead of a per click revenue, you receive a percentage of what the advertiser paid to have the ad placed. Instead of having a full advertisement, you will have a hyperlink to the Advertiser's homepage without any graphics. Basically, you as a website owner will sell smaller space to an Advertiser. Also, unlike Google AdSense, you get to approve or disapprove what ad link will be placed on your site.

You will get paid according to how your web**page**, not web**site**[3], is rated by a PR (Page Rank) score between 0

---

[3] Each time you navigate through a website, you are brought to an individual webpage.

and 10. This score is actually assigned by Google and dictates how important your web page is. As the score is assigned to each page of your website, you will have several PR scores for your entire webpage. The exact calculation of the score is kept secret by Google but generally the more pages you have linked to your page, a higher PR score will be achieved. Generally, the higher your PR score, the higher you will get paid for a text link ad.

There are a couple text link ad sites that will bring your site to the Advertisers. One is TNX (**www.tnx.net**) and another is Text Link Ads (**www.text-link-ads.com**). If you have a simple website, you may have a PR rating of 0. As such, TNX may be a better option as you can earn Advertiser's money irrespective of your PR rating. You can also sell link ad space for every page of your website.

If you have a blog, you can try to increase your PR rating by getting other blogs to link to your blog. Each post can be a different page to your website providing you with more opportunities to earn extra cash!

Let's Get Started:

- Go to TNX (**www.tnx.com**) or Text Link Ads (**www.text-link-ads.com**) and submit your website and blog. They need to approve the channel before they will advertise on your site.

Once approved, they will come to you with ads and ask you if you would like to proceed.

John Chow managed to profit over $2,000 in one month according to his September 2008 Blog Income Report! Not bad!

According to a personal study by Jim Karter (**www.jimkarter.com**), Internet Marketing Guru, text link ads can bring over **$3,000** per month[4]. In June 2006, he used the services of Text Link Ads for one page of his website. 3 months later, he expanded the link ads to other pages of this particular website to generate over $800 per month. Due to this success, he implemented the text link ads to his other websites. He earned over $3,000 in just 15 months of his trial! The following page provides an outline of his income activity.

[4] Source: http://www.jimkarter.com/2007-10-20-text-link-ads.html

The following provides an outline of Jim Karter's text link ad income:

Payment History

Date range:

| January (01) | 2006 | – | September (09) | 2007 | GO |

January 2006 - September 2007

Pay Period	Earning Amount	Payment Date	Check Amount
June 2006	$17.00	July 03, 2006	$17.00
July 2006	$17.00	August 01, 2006	$17.00
August 2006	$17.00	September 01, 2006	$17.00
October 2006	$275.58	November 01, 2006	$275.58
November 2006	$811.93	December 01, 2006	$811.93
December 2006	$1,284.17	January 01, 2007	$1,284.17
January 2007	$2,070.21	February 01, 2007	$2,070.21
February 2007	$2,512.41	March 01, 2007	$2,512.41
March 2007	$2,793.66	April 01, 2007	$2,793.66
April 2007	$3,096.53	May 01, 2007	$3,096.53
May 2007	$3,055.02	June 01, 2007	$3,055.02
June 2007	$2,931.86	July 01, 2007	$2,931.86
July 2007	$2,890.23	August 01, 2007	$2,890.23
August 2007	$2,987.20	September 01, 2007	$2,987.20
September 2007	$3,019.59	October 01, 2007	$3,019.59

* If you have any questions regarding payments or commissions, please send your inquiry to commissions@text-link-ads.com

Image Source: www.jimkarter.com

As you can see, it does not take long to earn decent income from text link ads.

"I try to do the right thing with money. Save a dollar here and there, clip some coupons. Buy ten gold chains instead of 20. Four summer homes instead of eight."

- LL Cool J

Chapter 6

Ebay – Unique Methods, Not Just Selling Unwanted Goods

Ebay has been a money maker for many. There are several books out there that will teach you to buy wholesale and sell the items for a markup. I will show you other methods that will earn you additional funds WITHOUT you having to hold inventory or having to bear sunk costs if no one purchases the product.

With each of the methods below, you will have to list the item first as a "Buy It Now" and once you have secured a bid and received payment, go and purchase the product to ship to your buyer!

a. Sell Items Unique in Your Area

The first method is to sell items that are only available in your area but cannot be purchased elsewhere. Don't buy the product yet! Try to take a picture of the item and list the item on ebay with your markup. You are trying to attract buyers who do not have easy access to this item. Only purchase the product and ship once you have secured a buyer and received payment from them.

You basically have no risk as you don't buy the item until it has sold.

Ideas for products that may be specific to an area: (a) Stores that are only in your city. For example, in my city, there is no ZARA (clothing store) and you cannot order online. However, I have made my purchases through ebay. The person selling probably made a nice profit from my purchase but I'm happy since now I can wear something I can't buy in my city! (b) Sports Jerseys! (c) Certain non-perishable food items, (d) collector pins, (e) souvenirs for major events held in your city.

b. Sell Items with Discounts Available to You

If you work for a large corporation, chances are there may be discounts available to you under an "Employee Purchase Program" (EPP). They usually allow such discounts to your organization as such an organization may purchase bulk units of their product. This discount will then be extended to the company's employees. The discount will depend on the type of agreement your employer will have with the store. You can usually find a listing of available discounts through your employer's internal website or call up some of the stores you are interested in and ask if they offer discounts to your company under an EPP. These discounts are usually offered to you and available even if you purchase it for friends and family.

If you DON'T have a discount through your employer, ask your friends and family to see if they have any discounts through THEIR employer. Perhaps you can give them a commission for using their discount. Otherwise, there may be other forms of discounts that YOU DO HAVE available such as: Student Discounts or Senior's Discount.

So, this is how you can make some money. Someone who does not have that discount will be willing to buy it from you as long as it is still lower than the retail price! In a way, you are splitting your discount between you and your buyer.

HERE'S HOW: List an item you have a discount on ebay as a "Buy It Now". You will add your profit to the discounted price but still keeping the price lower than the retail price. When you have a buyer, then you buy the item with your discount and have it shipped directly to your ebay buyer. Many places will offer free shipping online or you can charge the buyer the shipping and keep more profits. But there you have it, you will make money and you will have buyers as they will save money!

Let's Get Started:

We will use a real example through this section that I successfully executed through a well known computer manufacturer (let's call this store XYZ):

- Find out what discounts are available to you. As I mentioned, you can call the retail stores directly. Stores that may offer a discount to you would be: Apple Store, Panasonic, AT&T, GE, and Dell.

- At the time this guide was written, I could purchase a laptop from XYZ for $2449 through a dedicated employer discount link to their store. The same laptop sells on XYZ.com at regular retail price for $2799. That's a $350 difference!

- Research on ebay under the "Completed Listings" to see how much the item can sell for. I found out that the exact same Notebook sold for around $2650 - $2749.

- Decide on how much you want to list your item for. Remember to add the fees you will pay through ebay and paypal. I figured I will pay approximately $140 in transaction fees with the laptop. This will bring my total cost to $2590. I decided to list for $2700. This way, I will profit $110 but will still attract buyers as they will save $100 from buying from XYZ direct. I decided to indicate that any sales tax will be the responsibility of the buyer.

- Once you have listed your item and secured payment from a buyer, NOW go and purchase the item. In our example, I logged onto XYZ through my discount link and purchased the item as a gift and had XYZ ship directly to the buyer!

I've sold 7 units in the past month giving me an extra **$770**!

BONUS: Signup up for an airline frequent flyer credit card that will give a bonus of 15,000 bonus frequent flyer miles. Then use this credit card to purchase your discounted product (and all your other profit generating expenses, if any). Because you are paying for the product direct from the store, you get the miles! Assuming you receive 1 point per dollar, you can earn 2,800 miles for the laptop mentioned above. As an example, if you can complete 10 laptop transactions, you will have 28,000 miles – plus the 15,000 bonus miles! That's over **40,000 miles** – enough for a domestic round-trip ticket or in some cases, a one-way ticket across the ocean. IF you don't want the airline ticket, sell the miles on ebay and package it with another tangible product to sell for extra cash! At the time this manual was being written, 45,000 American Airline miles PLUS a key chain just sold for $576. That's **$1,676** in PROFIT (using the example of the 10 laptops for a $110 profit each and then selling the miles you earned from the transactions).

"If you really want to succeed, you'll have to go for it every day like I do. The big time isn't for slackers. Keep up your mental stamina and remain curious. I think that bored people are unintelligent people."

- Donald Trump

Chapter 7

Selling Information!

This income generating opportunity has GREAT POTENTIAL as the sky's the limit with this channel. EVERYONE has a hobby, talent, skill, or trade that they are good at and there is ALWAYS someone wanting to learn. You just have to find those people that you can market your hobby, talent, skill or trade to! It is quite easy to materialize a manual to show and teach someone how to do WHAT YOU CAN DO. Your profit margins will be HUGE with this as you should have little to no cost to create the product.

Not yet motivated to try this channel? Picture this: you write a manual and decide to sell for $20. Let's say you are able to sell 5 units per day, you will have $100 per day. If sales are stable, you will have earned **$3,000** in a month! If you keep your manual electronic, your cost to create this could be zero. As such, you just made a 100% pure profit of **$3,000**! Not convinced you can sell 5 units per day? I have a friend who sells different versions of workout books with images of exercises and workout logs. To make his product distinct from the rest, he used what some may think as "risqué images". Nevertheless, he made significant profits. He achieved sales of 75 units a day at $9.95, that's almost $750 per day – that's $22,500 per month!! Mind you he has binding costs of $2 per unit; still an 80% profit margin on $22,500 is still **$18,000**. Yes, he still maintains his primary job and only has his profits from the workout log as his supplemental income.

I will try to help you create an information product to sell and give you a guideline as to how you can develop and create your product. Then, I will show you ways you can sell and market your information product!

First, let's think of what information we can sell!

Let's Get Started:

- Create "List 1": List all the activities you enjoy doing, the skills you have, or life changing events that you have experienced. You are just brainstorming at this point so ensure you write down everything that comes to mind. Think of tasks you do at work and at home. Also, write down things you are interested in. I came up with the idea for this book as I listed "personal finance" as one of my interests. Some ideas:

- o If you traveled for a year around the world, you could put together a manual on navigation tips.

- o If you have a skill or hobby you can teach, you can create instructional DVDs or a manual – think of what you do on a daily basis that you might be taking for granted; managing a business, cooking specialty recipes, staying fit or keeping healthy, etc.

- Create "List 2": List all the groups of people you think you can belong to or that you understand well. Some examples include: young professionals, gay & lesbian, new parents, a particular ethnic group, stay at home moms, travel groups, etc. It is important to only write down groups you understand as this will give you a basis for your material.

- From "List 1", see if there is an activity that you can write about for a group in "List 2". The key at this point is to pick something you are interested in from the first list for a group that you would like to cater your product to. Your selection from "List 2" will now be your "target market"! Initially, you might think "why not sell to EVERYONE"? The problem with this is that you CAN'T satisfy everyone. You want to be able to develop your information so that a particular group can use it to their specific needs. This is finding your "niche" – the process whereby you are offering information that is not readily available to this group through specialization and customization.

- Read various articles and books on the subject to gain more knowledge. This will help you become an expert if you aren't already. If you are an expert on the activity you selected to write about, you can seek out your competition and try to put a different spin on the information you are going to provide.

- Talk to people and network – ask your friends if they are familiar with the topic. Ask them to provide you with ideas on the subject. I recommend not telling them you are writing a manual or planning to sell information as some may try and discourage you for whatever reason. I have heard many tell others that their product "won't sell" and the next thing you know they are bringing in thousands per month!

- From the above resources and combined with what you know, start making a bullet point list of topics related to your subject. If you are teaching someone how to do or make something, write the procedures or processes in order you would do them. If you are writing about an interest or hobby, try to sort your topics in some kind of order. This can now be your "Table of Contents".

- Now, fill in content under each bullet point. You can use any word processing system (i.e. Microsoft Word). At this point, just type whatever comes to mind. Keep typing, then edit later. For this book, I came back to edit two weeks later and managed to add more content after I took a two week break. I refined and revised more effectively after two weeks.

- **TIPS:** Still need ideas for what to write about, try searching "hot topics" or "best non-fiction sellers" – make a list of the references or books. Go to the book store and browse through the books to get inspiration and ideas for material.

- **TIPS:** Of course you can create the content yourself but if you need more help, think of topics that you enjoyed reading about in various articles and books. Take and combine key points from the various sources and **paraphrase.** By doing this, you are providing the buyer with a resource that you have already filtered out the useless or not so interesting information for them. Chances are if you aren't interested in other topics, they won't be since YOU

UNDERSTAND THEM – that's why you chose them as your "niche". Still need more information for your topics? No problem! Look for information in public websites not subject to copyright protection (such as government websites).

- **TIPS:** Add **BONUS** material to your creation to keep readers interested (and feel like they got their money's worth). It will help fill content as well.

- **MORE TIPS:** What?! You have NO time to find content for your money maker? No problem! Go to **www.elance.com** for virtual assistants. Do a search on "personal assistants" or "virtual assistants". It doesn't matter which country you are from, they have networks around the world. You can hire someone to do your research, content building, and then you just have to revise and put your name to it! The cost will range but you will find some assistants for as low as $4 per hour. Use the feedback feature to find a good assistant.

- Now that you have content, convert your word document into Adobe format so your buyers cannot edit it. To do this, go to Adobe Acrobat (**www.adobe.com**) to download a free version. At the top of your word processor, there should be a menu "Adobe PDF", once you click on the menu, an option should come up to "convert to

PDF". Select this option. You now should have a PDF version of your document.

- Use an on-demand publisher or go to CreateSpace (**www.createspace.com**) and have your material published. They will publish DVDs, CDs, Books, and Video. You submit your work and you will only get charged binding and print fees once someone orders your material. The fees are deducted from the selling price you set. The best part is that you will not have to worry about inventory costs! I strongly suggest this method. With CreateSpace, your item will automatically be listed on Amazon.com – think of your group of potential buyers through Amazon.com!

- If you decide to go with an on-demand publisher, find a graphic designer on Elance to have a cover professionally designed for your product. The cost for a good quality book cover will be approximately $100 - $130. Advise your designer that you are planning to publish on CreateSpace (or whichever publisher) and the designer can provide the design to you using the necessary template required by the publisher so all you have to do is upload it. Unless you are an expert in graphic design, it is strongly recommended that you hire a professional instead of trying to design this yourself as you want your product to be well packaged to attract buyers. IMAGE IS EVERYTHING and people DO judge a book by its cover!

- Use your free advertising channels mentioned in the earlier chapters to advertise your product. Ensure you promote your product using your website and blog.

- CreateSpace allows you to order your own product for a significant discount to the price you listed. Order a small amount of your product so you can list your item on ebay as a fixed item or "Buy It Now". Create multiple listings in various categories to allow your item to be searched under different means.

- If you don't want to use an on-demand publisher, you can list your item on ebay and indicate that you will mail a paper copy to the buyer. In some cases, ebay no longer allows you to list an item if only a PDF version is emailed.

- If you have multiple ideas, there is nothing to stop you from publishing different products! Multiply your income streams even more.

"Business is the art of extracting money from another man's pocket without resorting to violence."

—Max Amsterdam

Chapter 8

Keeping it Simple and Safe

CONGRATULATIONS on making it through the first 7 income streams to supplement your primary income. Hopefully by now, you have sufficient cash coming in. We want to start preserving your cash but at the same time have the money work for you to make more money! This section is more to prepare you for the last 2 income generating streams as they will require more funds for the initial investment. So when you're ready for the last two methods, you can just talk a walk to the bank. Right? Well, at least we can hope so.

I can advise you to go purchase some stocks and BOOM they can double in price! BUT if you read my Prelude, I have lost thousands in the stock market. I will strongly advise you to preserve your cash instead of investing in the stock market.

The rule in this section is Keep It Simple and **Safe** so please bear with me. There are many options out there but I would recommend either getting a Certificate of Deposit (CDs) or a Money Market Deposit Account (MMDA). Both are offered by most banks. As you continue to earn income from your different streams, keep adding the funds to your CD or MMDA until you have enough for the remaining income streams.

I will provide a brief outline of the two options here:

Certificate of Deposit:

- Requires a minimum deposit of $500 or $1,000.

- Requires you to leave your money untouched for a period of time (the longer you can leave it untouched, the more money you will earn).

- If you withdraw early, you may be charged a penalty which can be 50% of the interest you earned. Your original balance is always yours to keep; just a portion of the interest you earned is taken as a penalty if funds are withdrawn early.

- How much you earn depends on the bank's interest rate. You can go to **www.bankrate.com** for a listing of several banks that offer CDs and the rate you can receive. On the right of the website, you will see a filter in which you can apply to view rates for different types of CDs. At the time this guide was written, you can earn a 4% return.

Money Market Deposit Account:

- Usually requires a minimum deposit of $500.

- Earns less interest than a CD but allows more flexibility.

- Your money is never tied up and you can even write checks against your account without any penalty.

- How much you earn will depend on how much money you have in the account.

As you see, the amount of money you will make down this stream is quite low but the key is that these are low risk and will preserve your cash!

Taking it a step further, another way to make some extra cash for your long term benefit is tied to your retirement account (i.e. in Canada, your RRSP account and in the US, your 401(k)). Most employers will match your contributions up to a certain percentage in your retirement account. What this means is your company will put in the same amount of money in your retirement account that you put into your retirement account. If your company offers this program and you are not yet participating, SIGN UP IMMEDIATELY! I contribute $250 per month to my retirement account so my employer matches dollar for dollar – the full **$250** also! That's $3,000 extra they give me a year, add this to the

$3,000 I put in and assume it grows at a rate of 4% interest. That's another $240 in interest along with the $250 my employer contributed. In total, I will earn **$490** per month – automatically!

Let's Get Started:

- Open a CD or MMDA account with your preferred bank. Deposit any residual income you may have and start saving for the next income stream.

- Contact your employer and find out if they have a company match program for your retirement account. If they do, sign up and contribute the maximum amount they will contribute. The amount you want to contribute beyond this amount will depend on your age and situation which is beyond the scope of this manual. However, you can contact a Financial Planner to help you determine what your optimal contributions should be.

- In almost all cases, your employer will open the retirement account for you if you don't already have one. You just have to fill out the paperwork they give you.

- The payments and contributions will then be automatically deducted from your pay check.

Like I said earlier, it's automatic so you don't have to do anything else! Easy.

"The price of success is hard work, dedication to the job at hand, and the determination that whether we win or lose, we have applied the best of ourselves to the task at hand."

**- Vince Lombardi
American Football Coach**

Chapter 9

Be a Landlord

After I had implemented and improved the first few streams, I obtained a sufficient capital to purchase real estate. Now it can take some time to get here but don't give up. I opted to obtain a rental unit for my next flow of income. This is quite the investment but you will have a higher chance of getting a nice return for your money.

You may think that a rental unit is a significant investment beyond your means. However, it may actually be easier than you think. Depending on the area you live, you may need as little as 5% as a down payment. If you are looking at a 1 bedroom condo for $200,000 – you will only need $10,000 as a down payment. Of course, this depends on many factors to determine if you are able to qualify for a mortgage. You should contact a Mortgage Specialist or Mortgage Broker to determine your options.

If you own your own property, obtaining a deposit for a rental property may be easier than you think. If you have equity[5] built up in your current home, you can refinance your existing mortgage to pull out additional cash. Most people think they can only refinance only because they will receive a lower interest rate. However, you can also refinance to obtain more cash to put as a deposit on another piece of property. Although this will increase your new mortgage, you will now have two properties that have the potential to increase in value. This is called **LEVERAGING**. Usually, banks will require your home to have a market value of 25% more than your current mortgage value before allowing you to refinance for extra cash. Anything beyond the 25%, you will be allowed to obtain an additional mortgage for and use the extra capital to invest in additional property. At the time this book was being written, interest rates were at historical lows so refinancing to pull equity out may not cause your monthly payments to increase due. Again, you should contact your Mortgage Specialist or Broker to find out your options.

There are 3 different ways you can make money on a rental unit:

---

[5] Equity means that the price of your home has increased more than what you owe on your mortgage.

a. Month to Month Rental Income

The first way to make some money from your rental property is from the checks you receive from your tenant each month! If you are able to rent out your property for an amount enough to cover your expenses, you will net a profit each month.

b. Your Tenant Paying Down your Debt

As you receive your monthly rent payments, you will make payments towards your mortgage. Your mortgage payment will partly go to interest and the rest will be towards the principal balance (what is outstanding on your loan). As time goes on, what you will owe goes down as your renter is paying down your mortgage for you. Should you decide to sell, the less you have owing, the more you get to pocket!

Let's look at an example. Say you purchase a $220,000 home with a 10% down payment. You will have a mortgage of $200,000. Let's assume you find a tenant and sign a 1 year lease and decide to sell after the lease is up. For illustration purposes, we will also assume the price of the home remains at $220,000 after 1 year. After 1 year of payments, you will only owe $197,543. So if you sell the house at $220,000 and payback the $197,543 to your mortgage lender, you are left with $22,457. Of that, your initial investment was $20,000 – you just gained **$2,457**! This is because your tenants paid some of your principal for you!

c. Your Property Rising in Value

Real estate is cyclical meaning values will go up and go down. If you can time things right, you can purchase when housing prices are low and keep renting out the property until the prices go back up.

In the previous example, we assumed the price of the $220,000 did not change. However, say you rent out your unit for 2 years and housing prices increase a modest 6%. Before realtor fees, you will have gained **$13,200** in the two years.

Unfortunately, if you are the seller, you will have to pay realtor fees that will cut into this profit. I will provide more information in the "Let's Get Started" section regarding realtors and ways to reduce the realtor commissions so you can keep more profit.

So there you have it – **3 ways to make money by renting out property!**

There are a few reasons why real estate is a good source of income:

a. Provides a STABLE Form of Income

Once you sign a lease with your tenant, you can pretty much expect this amount from month to month. Also, you have some control over how much you can increase the rent by should your tenants chose to renew the lease.

- **TIPS:** My personal view is that I would rather have a good tenant than to keep increasing their rent. A good tenant will not complain as much and are low maintenance which will allow you to place more emphasis on other income generating streams. Also when screening tenants, ensure they have a good income so there won't be any late payments. I haven't received a late payment yet.

b. Low Maintenance

I was able to find a condo unit with an onsite maintenance person. Many have the perception that just because you are a landlord, you must deal with the fixing and repair requests. Fortunately, most condo units in the major cities will have an onsite maintenance person so you avoid such headaches.

c. Tax Benefits

Tax benefits will shelter your income as there are many tax deductible items that will help preserve your income. Most countries will allow you to deduct the following items: mortgage interest expense, property taxes, costs associated to finding your tenant (i.e. advertising), property management fees, and capital cost allowances. Capital cost allowance permits you to deduct a certain percentage of the original purchase price of your property as an "expense" from your rental income. This "expense" is only on paper for tax purposes to reduce your taxable income. If you have enough deductions, your rental income can pretty much be tax free. Tax rules will differ in each state or province and in each country so it is best to consult a Tax Specialist.

d. Capital Gains (or you can just call it PROFITS)

As I mentioned earlier, you have 3 ways in which to make money with a rental property. The capital gains can really be significant. You have heard how people have doubled their value of their homes! Your rental property has the potential to increase in value as well allowing you to capture the capital gains.

Let's Get Started:

Now I can't tell you where and what exactly to buy but hopefully I can present you with some tips I have learned along the way. This should help you in the decision making process.

- So how do you acquire property? At the time when I was purchasing and also while I was writing this manual, there were many deals around due to the financial crisis. I managed to purchase my first unit at a fantastic deal. I was able to take advantage of the low interest rates usually offered in a slow economy. This is a

HUGE investment so evaluate your situation before deciding to purchase real estate.

- Find and talk to a Mortgage Specialist or Broker. A mortgage broker acts as a middle-person between you and several banks. They can tell you how much of a loan you can get and what purchase price you can realistically look for. There are several Mortgage Brokers out there so talk to friends and family and try to get a referral. You should spend the time in looking for a good broker as when it is time to close on the property, he can help you get everything in order so you just have to sign papers.

- If you are willing to proceed with the purchase process and have the OK from the Mortgage Broker, it's time to go shopping! Write down a list of areas you would like to purchase in. Location is extremely important as this will determine if you have a good selection of quality renters. The location may also dictate what type of renter you will get. For example, if you are near a university, you may only get university students who may not be able to afford the rent or who may trash the place. Consider these items:

  o Accessibility to public transit lines towards downtown - you will get more young professionals that can afford rent but who may not be ready to purchase a place. They may be good long time quality tenants

o   Parks & dog parks – before you think "I don't want a dog in my unit", dog owners will bring you the cash!   AND LOTS OF IT!   I had originally planned to list my unit for rent at $1,300 per month but I was also near dog parks, bike paths, and a river. Initially, I had thought to put "NO DOGS" on my listing – but through word of mouth (a friend of a friend of a friend) had a dog and was desperately looking for a place. I got offered $1,600 if I was willing to rent her the place – and her dog! The offer came within a day. Many places will not allow dogs so dog owners have to pay a premium to get the places they want!

o   Gyms – I always get asked the question if a gym is close by so I'm adding it to the list.

o   Grocery stores, schools, etc – basically all other amenities you would look for when finding a place. You want to make sure that the property is highly desirable when it comes time to sell.

•   Find a realtor that specializes in the area you want to purchase in. They will be able to tell you if a property is over priced or not. If you are the buyer, using a realtor will be free to you (the seller pays them their commission).

- Work with your realtor to secure the purchase of your rental property. Your realtor will help you through the buying and closing process. Once you have a property in mind, contact your mortgage broker and he will guide you through the process to get a mortgage. There are a few products available and he or she can explain in detail the pros and cons of each. For my mortgage, I decided to use a line of credit (LOC) as opposed to the traditional mortgage[6]. The primary reason I chose this type of financing was because as you pay down your line of credit with your rental income, it frees up additional credit you can use to purchase your next rental property. The additional credit, in addition to the equity built up in my first unit, allowed me to purchase my second rental property a few months later! Also, you won't have to go through the whole approval process again to use available credit on your LOC.

- You will need a lawyer to handle the title transfer (to change the name of the property to yours). The legal fees range from $300 and up. Make sure you look around your area for a good one.

---

[6] Using a line of credit in place of a traditional mortgage may not be available in all States or countries. Your Mortgage Broker can advise you of what is available in your area.

There are also closing costs – this will range quite drastically depending on the country and state you live in. Your lawyer will be able to tell you in detail a summary of your closing costs.

- **TIPS:** Please bear with me a little in this section – this may sound confusing at first but there is a reason for this! When you are thinking of buying a rental property, you should have an open mind. Once you have purchased your property, I want you to turn around and list it as a rental AND AS a "FOR SALE". If you have the ability, stage the home a little different that when you purchased it. Bring some of your own furniture for staging – or just add a new coat of paint. Make it look a little different than when you purchased it. Take some good quality pictures (or have your realtor do this for you). Up the "FOR SALE" price by 12%. Take whichever offer comes first – either the rental or the purchase! The reason you want to up the "FOR SALE" price by 12% is so you can try to target an immediate 5 to 10% gain (depending on how you negotiate your realtor commissions when you sell – see next bullet point). The remaining 2% is to cover closing costs. You really have nothing to lose by listing it both ways. In fact, you will have more options to ensure your property is not just sitting there. Some buyers may view the place a little different if it has been staged or if there's a new coat of paint and may fall for the trap and BANG – you just made a 10% profit. If you get a renter first, that's fine too as this was your original intention. Some realtors will try to talk you out of listing it either way as they want whichever option brings them more commissions. If the realtors want your business they will have to abide by your rules and **DON'T let them talk you out of it.**

- SO, because you are going to immediately list the property as a "FOR SALE" after you purchase, you will advise your realtor that you will only hire them to purchase your rental property IF they give you a discount on their commission when you sell. Remember the seller pays the commission. Let them know your intentions to list your rental as a "FOR SALE" as well and that you will be taking whichever offer comes first. If they agree to give you a discount, get this in writing! Side note: you will be listing property as a rental with a **different** realtor but I will describe this more in detail further below.

- The entire closing process can take a week or longer depending on your situation. After you close, you will now find a tenant.

- You can chose to list the property yourself and do the advertising or you can hire a realtor that specializes in rentals. I chose to list my units myself on a local website that handles rentals. It took me a couple hours take a few pictures and to list my units for rent and show the units. I was able to rent the first unit out on the first day and the second unit in 3 days. If you prefer to use a realtor, use a different one that the one you select to list the property as a "FOR SALE". The reason being, realtors will get more commission if they complete a SALE than a rental. Using the same realtor for both may create situations where the realtor will not show you any interested renters – even if they come before the buyers.

- **TIPS:** Don't want to deal with the headaches of finding and dealing with a tenant? No problem. You can hire a property management company that will advertise your rental unit, screen applicants, find your tenant, and deal with all the paperwork. If any problems arise from the unit, you tenant will contact the property management company directly and the company will resolve everything for you. The fees range from 8% - 10% of the monthly rent plus any ad hoc costs that arise from your unit. There are several property management companies that operate in each city so you can do a search on the internet to find one you are comfortable with. Also, you can try **www.elance.com** to find cheaper independent Property Managers.

I currently have 2 rental properties. The first one I am renting out for $1,600 where my total expenses are

$1200 (mortgage payments, property taxes, condo assessment fees) providing me with a $400 profit per month. My second rental property I am renting out for $1650. Unfortunately, I wasn't able to find as good of a deal on the second unit so my expenses for my mortgage are a little higher at $1500. That still gives me a combined profit of **$550** per month! I would estimate that my first unit has appreciated $80,000 in value and my second unit has increased $30,000. I still have not sold so these gains are only unrealized. Until I sell, these appreciated values are only on paper and will not be realized until sold.

"Keep away from people who belittle your ambitions. Small people always do that, but the really great make you feel that you, too, can become great."

- Mark Twain

Chapter 10

Automation with Selling Products

In Chapter 7, I showed you how to sell information with low capital investment (money you put into to generate profits). In this section, we will explore ways to make money on tangible goods while keeping your investment and inventory costs low. Also, I will show you techniques on how to automate the process so you can keep your current job (this is all EXTRA CASH on top of your regular salary remember).

If you have a tangible item, there are a few different ways in which you can make money. You can sell it as is with a mark-up, modify it and have a mark-up, or invent something and take all the profits. If you chose to sell a product as is, your profit margins will not be as great. However, some prefer this route as this will be enough for them to earn their supplementary income. You can certainly import cheaper goods from countries such as India or China. By going this route, your shipping costs, import taxes, and inventory may become a heavy burden on you.

Here is where the automation will come in. Once you have figured out which product to sell, find out if the seller or manufacturer has a **drop-ship program** or a **fulfillment center**. Basically, a drop-shipment is when you order the goods from me, but I have my manufacturer send you the goods directly. I don't have to worry about storage costs or inventory. The best part is this: I only place the order to the manufacturer once I have received the order from you. As such, I only pay for the goods once I have a guaranteed buyer. A "fulfillment center" is the same idea. They handle the orders and ship them to your customers for you. You will also save on shipping costs as most of the centers have negotiated discounts with all the large shipping companies. You are just the middle-person that will collect the profits.

There is, however, a reason I decided to leave this income channel for the end. This does require MORE investment capital than the first stream. To have such a drop-ship program in place, the manufacturer or fulfillment center may ask for a deposit of $3,000 or more.

Let's Get Started:

- Go back to the lists you created in Chapter 7 – one in which you listed your interests and activities and the other with your potential niches. Create a third list of products that you can potentially sell to your niche. To help you, try to incorporate the list of your interests and activities.

- **TIPS**: When creating your third list of items to sell, consider items that may fill a need, something that people can't get as easily. As this is your final income stream, you should target a mark-up of 6 times your cost. This is higher than the industry recommendation of 5 times, but you will always have hidden costs to cover so we should bump this to 6 times.

- Think of items that are available in other countries but not in your own. Is it possible to modify the product without violating patent rights and have a modified product manufactured in your own country? This way, you can charge a premium as the product has been modified and also you don't have to worry about significant import costs.

- Once you have thought of an item to sell, calculate the total cost for you to purchase 1 of this item. Without purchasing the item, list the item on ebay as an auction to test the pricing. See if any bids come close to your mark up of 6 times the unit cost. Before the bid ends, end the listing.   Your task was only to determine the pricing. I would recommend doing this procedure a few more times and calculating an average price people are willing to pay for your item. If the bids come close to 6 times cost, CONGRATULATIONS – you are close to finding your product!

- Start contacting manufacturers and ask for quotes – there may be manufacturers out there willing to do it for less! Make sure they have a fulfillment center or drop ship program. It is a good idea to go in person and ask for discounts – they may find it harder to say no in person. If you don't have time to run around, no worries! Let's go back to **www.elance.com**. You might be able to find a personal assistant that can do the leg work for you at a cheap price.

- Set up an online store at Yahoo Stores (**www.smallbusiness.yahoo.com/ecommerc e**).   It will cost you approximately $40 per month, however, the ease of setting it up and convenience will make it worth while. Also, they charge less selling fees than ebay. Through the Yahoo Store, you can accept both credit card and paypal payments. Or find a website designer on **www.elance.com** – depending on your website needs, you may be able to have one designed and developed for $300.

- START SELLING! Now that you have an online store, you want to advertise. Since you now know how to use Google Adwords, you can bring traffic to your website. Remember, you can use other tools I have presented to you earlier such as issuing a press release.

- Consider alternate advertising channels to increase your product sales such as local magazine publications. Use your income earned from previous channels to run print or radio advertising.

As I mentioned at the beginning of this chapter, there is great income generating potential with this technique. An example may motivate you to explore this channel more seriously. Timothy Ferriss is founder of BrainQUICKEN LLC (**www.brainquicken.com**) and was as one of Fast Company's "Most Innovative Business People of 2007"[7]. He started his business with $5,000 but he went from earning $40,000 per year to making **$40,000** per month as a result of BrainQUICKEN. A drop shipment program was used so that Timothy does not require any inventory on hand for his products. Once the items are ordered by the customer, the products are sent directly to the buyer. He has also outsourced functions of his business so the process is automated. More information can be found on his blog at the URL provided in the footnote below.

[7] Source: Timothy Ferriss,
http://www.fourhourworkweek.com/blog/about (2008)

There is so much potential out there and there will always be buyers. The hardest part is finding the item that they will buy! However, that is half the battle. Keep reviewing your lists created in the "Let's Get Started" sections. Your idea may not come to your immediately but if you are dedicated, I am confident that you will find an idea. Keep your lists with you when you travel abroad as other cultures have great ideas and products that could always be brought home.

If you still need some help with ideas, consider these resources:

- WorldwideBrands (**http://worldwidebrands.com**) – offers a wide range of drop shipment products. Browse through their product listing and find a product that you can work with. They can assist with market research as well.

- If you want to sell brand name products, take a look at Simplx.com (**http://www.simplx.com/**) – most products on their website will offer a drop shipment program. The problem with brand name products is that you may not get your desired mark-up of 6 times cost.

Bonus Material

Money Savings on Credit Card BONUS: If you have balances carried on your credit card and have maintained a good history of on-time payments, you can actually reduce the interest rate on your card simply by calling your credit card company. Ask them if you qualify for a lower interest rate. Usually, you will need to be a customer for at least one year and you can keep doing this every 6 months.

50% Savings on Travel BONUS: After completing the income generating methods in this book, I hope you now have some money to travel. But you still want to be cautious with your money. Here's how to save 50% on your hotel and airfare:

For Airfare:

- Use ITA Software Trip Planner (**http://matrix.itasoftware.com**) to research the cheapest flights available on the dates you would like to travel.

- If you are going to Europe from North America, compare the above fare with 1-800-FLY-EUROPE (**www.1800flyeurope.com**).

- Orbitz (**www.orbitz.com**) often offers online promo codes that can be found by performing an online search. Compare the Orbitz price, with the discount or promo code if available, with the above.

- Take the lower price of the above and go to Priceline (**www.priceline.com**) and start your bid at 50% of the lower price and move up in your desired increments.

As a side note, you don't always have to book in advance; there can be last minute sales available.

For Hotels:

- Go to Bidding For Travel (**www.biddingfortravel.com**), an online forum that discloses what hotel you are likely to get in each category on Priceline and at what price. Research the prices awarded through Priceline. Don't forget to post what you have won on Priceline and **include a link to your websites and blog**!

- Compare the above prices with a travel search engine like SideStep (**www.sidestep.com**). This search engine will search numerous hotel websites for you and present the lowest priced options for you.

- Perform an online search of hotel promo codes. Hotels are always offering discounts to lure travelers especially when the economy is not doing well.

- Also, your employer may have an agreement with the hotel chain you are looking to book. Contact the hotel directly – NOT through the 1-800 number. Ask for "in-house reservations" and identify yourself as an employee of your company. Ask if there are special corporate rates available. If you work in the travel industry (airline, hotel, travel agent, tour groups), chances are you will get 50% off the rack rate.

Or if you want to save even more on your travels, the following sites allow you to find free accommodations:

For Free Accommodations:

- Check out this website - Global Freeloaders (**www.globalfreeloaders.com**) – is an online community that allows you to find free local accommodations. It also allows you to meet new local friends that may show you around as well.

- Or for a more long term option - Home Exchange International (**www.homeexchange.com**).

Time Saving BONUS: Using Pareto's 80/20 Rule, you can save time in your primary job to create additional time for your income streams. If you aren't familiar with Pareto's Rule, it basically states that 80% of results come from 20% of efforts. In other words, you should be able to condense your current work into less time and still have the same output.

To assist with identifying what to condense, write down all the tasks you do at work. Under each task, write down the steps that are required for you to deliver the result. Think of any steps that can be eliminated or combined that produce the same result. Are there steps that take up most of your time but only contribute to less than 5% of the deliverable? What if you eliminated this time consuming step and produced 95% of the deliverable? Will anyone notice that less than 5% of the deliverable is missing? Perhaps the 5% was not required or no one ever cared for this remaining 5% component. If such steps exist, it may be a good idea to try and eliminate such steps to become more efficient and free up time.

Blog BONUS: No time to build a blog? You can find someone to build your blog through Elance!! I purposely left this for later in the manual as I am hoping you can now afford some of these services using the income you generated from the previous streams.

"Many of life's failures are people who did not realize how close they were to success when they gave up."

- Thomas Edison

Ending Remarks

Once again I would like to thank you for purchasing this book. I truly hope you have found valuable information here that will help you earn additional income.

I would also add that to achieve the results I have attained, there has been more effort on my part to make it work; this is not a quick make money solution. There needs to be effort, dedication, and risk taking! If you do not explore and try new options, you will never get to the point of making thousands per month in supplementary income.

I wish each of you all the best in your future endeavors.

Good Luck.

Marc Gaudet.